MARKEDA JOHNSON

OPEN EYE'S DAILY DEVOTIONAL

OPEN EYE'S

DAILY DEVOTIONAL

MARKEDA JOHNSON

OPEN EYE'S: DAILY DEVOTIONAL

MARKEDA JOHNSON

Printed in the United States of America

Catalogued in the Library of Congress

ISBN- 13:978-1719242561
ISBN- 10:1719242569

Published by:
True Faith Consulting & Publishing

Unless otherwise noted, all Scripture quotations are taken from the English Standard Version of the Bible.

DEDICATION

This book is especially dedicated to every person who didn't have a plan....But the plan was revealed through His Plan.

For I know the plans I have for you
"declares the Lord,"
Plans to prosper you and not harm you, plans to give you hope and a future.

~Jeremiah 29:11~

TABLE OF CONTENTS

ACKNOWLEDGEMENT

First given honor to God my LORD and Savior Jesus Christ which is the head of my life. I thank God for my divinely appointed helpmate and shepherd Larry L. Johnson. WE have seven spirit-filled children Tyree, Catrine, Saraya, Kelarriea, Nicholas, Arianna, and Makalia; they are all indeed blessings to me. Thank God for the prophetic role of my Father, Brothers, Sisters, Mother and Father-in-law.

My heartfelt gratitude to all, particularly Dr. S' Jerry & Chandris McCoy, Minister Patricia Taylor, Minister Dorothy A. Moore, Angela Moore, Bill Lamar, Elgie Loyd and so many other individuals and friends who stood by me through this journey. I'm blessed and privilege to be the Elect Lady of Haven's Believers Outreach Ministry in Dallas, TX of a loving, prayerful church. I value the support in spirit, deed, cash and kindness which all of you have contributed, and it will always remain deep in my heart. May God bless you all, in Jesus Name.

1

FOLLOW
THE
LEADER

"FOLLOW THE LEADER"
1 King 2:3

And, keep the charge of the Lord your God. Walking in his ways and keeping his statues, his commandments, his rules, and his testimonies as it is written in the Law of Moses, that you may prosper in all that you do and wheresoever you turn. We must obey and have "Open Eyes" to follow God's command because our life and others are depending on it. If we are not obedient then we can end up harming others which means if the Lord gives you instructions and you rebel against him then you have sinned. God has kept his promises and we must do the same rather its personal, conditional or unconditional; just like God, we should honor and obey him. Disobey and be punished. God is the one in control always remember that he has the last say; not us.

"MONKEY SEE MONKEY DO"
2 Chronicles 20:35

After that Jehoshaphat, King of Judah joined with Ahaziah, King of Israel, who acted wickedly. Don't be a partaker by participating or going along with others that will allow you to sin and be foolish. Instead have "Open Eyes" and partake in the victory of the attributes of Christ with wisdom. It's easy to indulge in ugly jokes or to get yourself involved with people who will try to manipulate you to sin, for it is truly the trick of the enemy and before you know it you'll be talking about others, judging them and have caused them to pressure you to be worldly, just as monkey see; monkey do. But remember, you must suppress the flesh daily and walk by faith and not by sight, for man will lead you wrong, but the spirit of the Holy Ghost will keep you for falling.

"I MADE IT WITH MY GOOD EYE"
Matthew 10:1

And He called to him his twelve disciples and gave them authority over unclean spirits, to cast them out, and to heal every disease and every affliction. Jesus called Peter, John, James, Matthew, Judas, Andrew, Zebedee, Bartholomew, Thomas, Simon, Thaddaeus and Phillips. Jesus called the twelve disciples because he trusted them, and he knew they trusted him. They had seen the miracles he had performed on people. He gave them pacific instructions on what to do. Once you are born again and are free indeed, you no longer make decision on your own understanding. God orders your steps and leads you with his Spiritual eye which means he instructs you on what to do and where and which way to go. All you must do is trust in him with your whole heart and have "Open Eyes" to see. Just like the disciples trusted Jesus.

2

FASTING AND PRAYING FOR PROTECTION

"FASTING AND PRAYING FOR PROTECTION"
Ezra 8:21-23

Then I proclaimed a fast there, at the river Ahava, that we might humble ourselves before our God, to seek of him a straight way for us. Fasting and praying for protection is a sacrifice you give unto the Lord. It also build's a relationship with you and God. You are killing the flesh and living by the Spirit. The Lord will sustain you in your time of need but the only way to get through it is prayer and fasting. He will build a fence around you and protect you, your family, your life, body and soul. All you must do is trust in Him; and have "Open Eyes" to see because the journey gets rough, but the power of God will bring his wrath upon anyone who thinks they're going to harm His children. Dear God, I ask you to protect me and my family from all the workings of the strongholds that are against us and our finances; and bless all that is good in the name of Jesus, Amen!

"THE LORD IS MY LIGHT AND SALVATION"
Psalm 27:1

The LORD is my light and salvation: whom shall I fear? The LORD is the strength of my life of whom shall I be afraid? Fear is a dark shadow that envelopes us and ultimately imprisons us with ourselves. Each of us have been a prisoner of fear at one time or another. We fear rejection, loneliness, uncertainty, sickness, loss of jobs, divorce, failure, misunderstanding, and even death; but by prayer and fasting we can conquer fear with "Open Eyes" as we see God's protection working in our lives to offer us help for today and hope for the future with unwavering confidence as an antidote to dispel fear and darkness all around us. So, let us always remember, the LORD is our light and our salvation, whom shall we fear, and whom shall we be afraid.

"GOD WILL SHOW YOU THINGS"
Daniel 8: 4-8

As with Daniel God will show you things that will happen at an appointed time weather it is in a dream or if he speaks it through his word. People allow their minds to make them believe that they are great in Power but to only see that it's not the power of God but man. Destruction from cunning and deceit prosperity under your own hand can destroy many lives, and an unclean situation can have an unhealthy effect on a long turn destination. I encourage you to seek the truth of God and his Word through "Open Eyes" with fasting and praying; that you may find strength for your journey and ask God to show you the vision and the plans he has for your life.

3

TODAY IS MY DUE DATE

"TODAY IS MY DUE DATE"
Judges 13: 3-5

And, the angel of the Lord appeared to the woman and said to her, behold you are barren and have not borne children, but you shall conceive and bear a son. Therefore, be careful and drink no wine or strong drink and eat nothing unclean, for behold you shall conceive and bear a son. Samson was to never cut his hair or eat anything unclean nor his mother because she had to be pure for the seed to produce good fruit. Pregnancy is 9 months and then the child will be delivered into this world. Can you also be pregnant in the Spirit? Yes; God can poor his word into you and in a 9-month time frame allow you to deliver His word to the people just as he gave it to you. But, at the same time we too, must give a sacrifice unto the Lord; as with "Open Eyes" to show that you can be trusted with his people, because the Holy Ghost can't dwell in an unclean spirit.

"DON'T BLAME IT ON THE NEXT MAN"
Luke 17

Temptations to sin are sure to come, but Woe to the one through whom they come! It would be better for him if a millstone were hung around his neck and he were cast into the sea than to cause one of these little ones to sin. So, pay attention to yourselves with "Open Eyes" and if your brother sins, rebuke him and if he repents, forgive him and if he sins, against you seven times in the day and turns to you seven times saying I repent you must forgive him. For instance, if a little girl comes up to her mother and say's my friend said people who smoke are stupid what do you say? Do you respond; your friend is right they are stupid? And, if the child says, well my dad smokes and my auntie smokes too; are they stupid? What do you say now that you have drawn them into temptation to sin against someone who has authority over them? Choose your words carefully, that you sin not.

And, be careful not to point your finger at other people's mistakes because there are three pointing back at you. Now, aren't you glad we have God's mercy upon us? So, remember, if your brother curses you out and then come and say, "I'm sorry" but minutes later curse you out again, and then five minutes later say, "I'm sorry" once more; you must forgive him. Likewise, if your new boyfriend has been taking you over to his ex-girlfriend's brother's house for almost a year and later you learn that the guy is his ex-girlfriend's brother and it angers you; when he comes and ask you to forgive him, then you must forgive him. Just as Jesus forgives us daily for our sins, we must also forgive others. It's important, to love one another the way Jesus loves us that we fall not for the adversary's foolishness; and sin not.

4

WOULD YOU DO THAT FOR ME

"WOULD YOU DO THAT FOR ME"
2 Corinthians 8: 16-17

But, thanks be to God who put into the heart of Titus the same earnest care I have for you. For he not only accepted our appeal but being himself very earnest he is going to you of his own accord. When you became a child of God he gives you a renewed mind and a clean heart which means the same love He abides in you should be given to others as a gift without repentance. If someone comes to you and tell you that they are sick with Cancer and may have already had other medical problems that they overcame but now sickness occurs again. Would you be able to stand in the gap like Jesus did for us and love your neighbor enough that you would ask God to take you as a sacrifice for them to be healed (with a pure acceptance in your heart that God was going to do it). Could you do that for someone? Try "Open Eyes" to see the goodness of God's Mercy.

"I AIN'T TO PROUD TO BEG"
2 Chronicles 24: 12-13

And, the King and Jehoiada gave it to those who had charge of the work of the house of the Lord, and they hired masons and carpenters to restore the house of the Lord, and also workers in iron and bronze to repair the house of the Lord. So, those who were engaged in the work labored and the repairing went forward in their hands, and they restored the house of God to its proper condition and strengthen it. Don't be ashamed in what God is doing in your life. Through "Open Eyes" speak with boldness to others about doing his will. You can't assume who you think might do the will of God. Therefore, get out and ask people to help raise money for the church or ministry you serve. Don't limit the Lord or who can help but rather Evangelize and tell others; and you may be surprise of how many people will follow if you lead by example.

"IN GOD WE TRUST"
1 King 17: 8-9,13

Then the Word of the Lord came to him arise go to Zarephath, which belongs to Sidon and dwell there. Behold, I have command a widow there to feed you. And Elijah said to her "Do not fear, go and do as you have said. But first, make me a little cake of it and bring it to me and afterwards make something for yourself and your son." When the Lord spoke to Elijah to go to Zarephath he didn't question the Lord, but he went and did according to the word of the Lord. Meaning he trusted in God and had no fear in his heart. If you trust in the Lord with all your heart and lean not to your own understanding, then he will direct your path in all the ways of your life. If God says quite your job and you know you heard it from Him; trust that you know that everything will be alright, even if it doesn't make sense to you at the time. Trust and "Open Eyes" will help build your faith and show your compassion towards Christ.

5

SUPER-
NATURAL
MEDICINE

"SUPERNATURAL MEDICINE"
Jeremiah 30:13

There is none to uphold your case, no medicine for your wound; no healing for you. We as Christians can have sin and iniquity in our hearts from unforgiveness, anger, frustration and a multitude of other things as we try to overlook our own sins. It's always easy to find fault in someone else, but we must have "Open Eyes" and be aware of putting our confidence in useless cures while our sins spread and cause us pain. A disease cannot be properly treated without the correct treatment. Jesus alone can cure the disease of sin. There is a "balm in Gilead" but you must be willing to let him do it. Trust that God will heal your open wounds and fill them with his love and kindness.

"RESCUE 911"
Psalm 42:4

These things I remember as I pour out my soul. How I would go with the throng and lead them in procession to the house of God with glad shouts and songs of praise; a multitude keeping festival. God is saying he is here to rescue you and is calling you to worship him and to always give confession of your sins. The Lord wants you to be encouraged and trust him for every hurt or pain caused by slander from friends, family and others; and through prayer and worship he will restore you. Don't be discourage but meditate on God's goodness and let him give you the ability in-order to help you rather than you trying to do it yourself. Call on Him daily (even through "Open Eyes") and he will come to your rescue.

"WITH JUSTICE FOR ALL"
Deuteronomy 24:16

Fathers shall not be put to death because of their children, neither shall the children be put to death for their fathers; but each one shall be put to death for his own sin. People tend to treat the poor and the oppressed as if they are not worthy of God or incompetent. More so, it may be the circumstance that caused them to be at a state of poverty-stricken. No-one is perfect, so, instead of trying to rob the poor or be oppressed from the little that they may have we should help them fix their situation by proving them with help, food, shelter or praying words of advice and much more. With "Open Eyes" we can treat them fairly and do our part to see that their needs are met; this is true justice for all.

6

GRANTED OUT OF GOOD WILL

"GRANTED OUT OF GOOD WILL"
2 Kings 22:6

This is to the carpenters and to the builders, and the masons and let them use it for buying timber and quarried stone to repair the house. God does not trust everyone. Just because you are a Pastor, or a Deacon of the church don't mean you are to be trusted with everything. This can mean in several aspects; rather it's, finances, healing, or prophecy to others. They were given instructions to give the money to certain people for a reason. They dealt honestly and when you are like this in the sight of God, then he will grant you favor over your life which is far more better than silver and gold. Serve the Almighty diligently; don't rob him of his riches and be a good steward over what he has blessed you with. With "Open Eyes" taste and see that the Lord is good.

"WONDERFUL COUNSELOR
Romans 11:34

For who has known the mind of the Lord or who has been his counselor? God owes no explanation to anyone. For He is the creator of all things and the Author and Finisher of our Faith. In other words, just because you don't understand him does not mean He is wrong. We as human beings must realize that we are unable to give advice to God or criticize his ways. God has absolute power and wisdom over us. Never think you can out think or out smart God because he knows your thoughts from afar. Even through "Open Eyes" or in that very moment when you think you got it all together, He will remind you that he is the one in control, so, stop trying to figure him out and just trust Him in all your ways that he may direct your path.

"THE HELP"
Exodus 22:21

You shall not wrong a sojourner or oppress him, for you were sojourners in the land of Egypt. When you move to a new city, town or country it feels a bit strange to adjust to that atmosphere. And if you're from another country you might have to learn another language to understand the people or be able to cope with society. This is how it is when you come into the realm of Christ. Trying to learn the difference between Satan's voice; God's voice; and your conscious can be challenging. It can also be frustrating if you have told someone something and (said you heard from God) but it doesn't come to pass. This is when the gift of discernment comes into place. It could or could not have been Him. So, make sure you are understanding toward others and their feelings; and exercise "Open Eyes" to help learn God ways; that you may help another.

7

HUMILITY

"HUMILITY"
Philippians 2:3

Do nothing from selfish ambition or conceit, but in humility count others more significant than yourself. Your ideas and your neighbor's interest might be different from one to another. But, as a Christian you should be mindful and humble yourself not to speak out of character. Humility shows your love for Christ. Jesus went through humility even though he knew he was God in the flesh, and he died a humiliating death (even death on the cross) not counting himself better then others. God might give you a vision, dreams, and even the gift of being a prophet, but even with that, you should encourage others and have their best interest at heart; as with "Open Eyes" because when it's all over every knee shall bow and every tongue shall confess that Jesus Christ is Lord, in Heaven and on Earth; and to Him be the Glory.

"FAITHFULNESS"
2 Samuel 24: 12-14

Thus, says the Lord, three things I offer you, choose one of them, that I may do it to you. So, God came to David and told him and said to him "Shall three years of famine come to you in your land? Or will you flee three months before your foes while they purse you? Or shall there be three days pestilence in your land. Now consider and decide what answer I shall return to him who sent me. Then David said to God, I am in great distress. Let us fall into the hand of the Lord for his mercy is great but let me not fall into the hand of man. The Lord will take you throw the wilderness but when he brings you out he will make you whole. God knows how to get your attention that will make you know that he is God, and God alone. No matter rather it's the good times or the bad; trust in the Lord, even through, "Open Eyes" and he will increase your faith.

"IDOLATRY"

1 Corinthians 10: 18-22

Consider the people of Israel; are not those who eat the sacrifices participants in the altar? What do I imply then? That food offered to idols is anything or that an idol is anything? No, I imply that what pagans sacrifice they offer to demons and not to God. I do not want you to be participants with demons. Pursue "Open Eyes" because you cannot drink the cup of the Lord and the cup of demons. You cannot partake of the table of the Lord and the table of demons. Shall we provoke the Lord to jealousy? Are we stronger than He? You cannot serve two masters. Nor live a lukewarm life. You can't serve Satan on Saturday in the club and praising God on Sunday in the Church saying you are Christian. For there is no temptation that has over taken you that is not common to man. God is faithful, and he will not let you be tempted beyond ability, but with the temptation he will also provide the way of escape, that you may be able to endure it.

8

SPIRITUAL HEALING AND MIRACLES

"SPIRITUAL HEALING AND MIRACLES"

John 5: 9-17

And, at once the man was healed and he took up his bed and walked. See you are well! Sin no more, that nothing worse may happen to you. Some people are ill physically and spiritually and because they have not asked God for forgiveness of their sins He want allow them to be physically healed. There is some deliverance that must take place in man for God to perform a miracle. The Sabbath day was Holy, but Jesus was still preforming miracles. When God heals you he not only heals the outer appearance, but he heals your inner man to make a complete transformation. Jesus heals to set man free and forgives him of his sins. The Lord is still doing miracles in people's lives today, so don't allow what it looks like now to hinder you from a blessing that is awaiting your acceptance. "Open Eyes" will help you see God's Spiritual Healing and Miracles.

"SEEKING"
Exodus 13:11

When the Lord brings you into the land of the Canaanites as he swore to you and your fathers and shall give it to you. God made a promise unto us saying that if we are willing and obedient than we will eat good of the land, and if I pray for my neighbor (through "Open Eyes) to be healed, and believe in my heart, God will do it. And, when we obey and sacrifice He will rewarded our good works and it will bless us and others as well.

"LIFE IN THE SPIRIT"
Romans 8: 1-11

With life in the Spirit; there is no condemnation of those who are in Christ Jesus. Jesus condemned sin in the flesh when he died on the cross. So, don't walk or set your mind on things of the flesh but of the Spirit. Money, cars and jobs are of the flesh. Life, Peace, Joy, Love, Kindness, and Self-Control are things of the Spirit, and through these He will give life to our mortal bodies; with "Open Eyes" to praise Him.

"DO NOT FAINT"
Mark 8:3

And, if I send them away hungry to their homes they will faint on the way and some of them have come from far away. I once had $25.00 in my account with less than a half of tank of gas in my car while traveling from one city to the next; and I had 5 children to feed. When I got home I still didn't know what I was going to do, but then I got a knock on the door and as I open the door, a man asks, "can your husband take me to the store and I'll give him $20.00?" then he said, "no, I'll give him $25.00 and put some gas in your car." God's word says, "I will never leave you or forsake you." That day, we were able to feed our family and had food left-over. If God fed four thousand people with four loaves of bread and a couple of fish; what more will He do for us? God will not let those who trust in him faint. Therefore, with "Open Eyes" we will walk and not be weary; we will run and not faint; and we will mount up with wings like Eagles as we wait on our Lord.

9

WHY

ME

"WHY ME"
Matthew 27:17

"Whom do you want me to release for you, Barabbas or Jesus who is called Christ?" Sometimes people who see potential in you will act evil toward you for no reason at all. They will have the attitude that they don't like you, but they can't tell you why. At this point it becomes envy which is a sin in God's eye. The people wanted to let a prisoner go and kill Jesus. But, why would you want to allow something that is corruptive to yourself or others be open to you? This is the same as sin. Remember, we have a choice to choose to do what is right, so with "Open Eyes" we can learn to obey God and rebel against sin as we surrender to his righteousness.

"VICTORY IS MINE"
Jeremiah 50:1

The word of the Lord spoke concerning Babylon, concerning the land of the Chaldeans by Jeremiah the prophet; Declare you among the nations and publish, and set up a standard. Sometimes it seems like it's almost impossible to get through a storm when you have been going through it for so long. But God comes in right on time and shows His faithfulness. There is nothing too hard for God. After He gets you through and you began to walk on dry land he then makes your enemy your footstool and allows you to gain victory. The day will come when there will be no evil upon us once and for all. Because vengeance is mine; declares the Lord. So, have "Open Eyes" to see what the prophet says, and join yourselves to God with an everlasting covenant that shall not be forgotten.

"WHEN YOUR LIFE SEEMS TO BE FALLING APART"
Isaiah 61:7

Instead of their shame there shall be a double portion. Instead of dishonor they shall rejoice in their portion, therefore in their land they shall possess a double portion and they shall have everlasting joy. God doesn't always take us out of a situation, but he will see us through it. Ask God to comfort you as you face the problems of life. Prayer changes things and when you see your brother is troubled, pray for him to gain strength through Christ Jesus. And, as you pray with "Open Eyes" for them, this will also open a door for yourself as God gives you a double portion. He will poor out his tender love and mercy that will comfort you daily through His word and make an everlasting covenant with you, and your seed shall be known among the nations.

10

I

PLEAD

MERCY

"I PLEAD MERCY"
Psalm 106:23

Therefore, he said he would destroy them had not Moses, his chosen one stood in the breach before him to turn away his wrath from destroying them. Moses served as the people's intercessor to prevent God's wrath to come upon them. Have you every interceded for someone to ask God to have mercy upon their soul. We can pray to God to use us to bring others into right relationship with him. But they must ask for forgiveness and change from their wicked ways. God will fulfill his promises once we change to show us how merciful he is. Although no man is righteous he is willing to forgive and restore us to himself. So, stand in the gap for others with "Open Eyes" to help show them how merciful our God is when you receive and obey him. Repent and turn from your wicked ways and He will poor out a blessing you want have room to receive.

"I DON'T NEED A REASON TO PRAISE"
Psalm 104:9

You set a boundary that they may not pass, so that they might not again cover the earth. God created the heavens and earth and all that is in it. I find it a joy to see how the trees and the water praise him and how the animals obey his commands; neither the trees or the animals go without nourishment, and the waters know their boundaries. But as people we can't find the time to just praise God for all he has done and is doing in our lives. There are evil forces that walk this earth but there are also angles from above that walk the earth as well. Praise God during a storm and praise him for new mercies offered to you every day. Praise Him with song, dance and "Open Eyes". Our blessings are from our praise, so give thanks unto the Lord of Host, give thanks unto his Holy name. Today, tomorrow and always I will Praise His Holy name.

"EVERYONE MAKES MISTAKES"
2 Corinthians 2:5

Now if anyone has caused pain, he has caused it not to me, but in some measure -not to put it too severely -to all of you. In God's eye we are all sinners but when we come to him in repentance he forgives us of our sins. So why don't we forgive others when they sin against us? We say with our mouth we have forgiven but our hearts reflect, we have not; rather it's the preacher who humiliated you in front of the congregation, or if it's the wife or husband who cheated and committed adultery against you. Avoid mistakes in discipline as a church or a Christian by being too harsh, angry or with unforgiveness when correction occurs. We must forgive others, for all have sinned and fallen short of God's mercy. Offer "Open Eyes" with leniency; and always remember there is a time to comfort and a time to correct, but in all you do, do it with Love.

11

HE PAID MY COVER CHARGE

"HE PAID MY COVER CHARGE"

Leviticus 16"10

But the goat on which the lot fell for Azazel was to be presented alive before the Lord to make atonement over it, that it may be sent away into the wilderness to Azazel. Jesus Christ died for our sins so that we don't have to be condemned. Our sacrifice is to obey, believe, and trust by faith. Once we go to God and ask for forgiveness we must realize that he at that moment forgives and forgets. We do not have to bring it back up to him again because we are cleansed and washed by the blood of Jesus. This is not to say we must go to God unprepared and careless, but we must honor him and prepare our hearts as we draw near in prayer. Have "Open Eyes" and forgiving hearts so our guilt and sins are forgiven by putting our trust in Christ. He is the only one who can set us free, and who Jesus has set free; is free indeed.

"JESUS WILL MAKE A WAY"
John 2:3-5

When the wine ran out the mother of Jesus said to him, "They have no wine," and Jesus said to her, "Woman, what does this have to do with me? My hour has not yet come." His mother said to the servants, "Do whatever he tells you." When you can't figure out why somethings are the way they are, and you know you're doing God's will. All you must do is trust in the Lord. If you can't understand then sometimes the Lord wants you to see that; He is God and God alone. When we bring our problems to the Savior we might think of ways he should handle it, but he may have a completely different outlook on things. Trust that God will deal with your problems as He see fit. Have "Open Eyes" to see in the Spirit and know God's children never go lacking nor will he leave you or forsake you; so, trust in Him and him alone for he will always make away.

"GET ON MY LEVEL"
John 11:42

I knew that you always hear me, but I said this on account of the people standing around that they may believe that you sent me. Those which are dead in the flesh Christ brought back to life. God's word brings in the light and reveals the darkness, so the soul can begin to cry out unto the Lord. If we take Christ word and rely on his power and faithfulness we shall see the glory of God. We cannot convert our relatives or friends, co-workers or neighbors; but we should warn them and invite them to Christ. Offer them "Open Eyes" and continue to pray for them all. This will pull down the strongholds of Satan and his evil forces. It will remind them and let them know that Jesus came to give us life and life more abundantly. Therefore, over-come your infirmities and allow Jesus to take control. Coming together on a Christian level, for your sake and my sake with Christ forever.

12

IT'S THE END OF THE NEW BEGINNING

"IT'S THE END OF THE NEW BEGINNING"
Leviticus 23:21

And you shall make a proclamation on the same day. You shall hold a holy convocation. You shall not do any ordinary work. It is a statue forever in all your dwelling places throughout our generations. When we walk into our season we must realize that there must be growth taken place at that time of harvest and that we must overcome the storms, rains, heartaches and pain. In order for the wheat to be produced the barley must ripen first. The wheat shows that the barley made it through and now the harvest can continue to proceed. So, rejoice that you are an overcomer in God's eye and give him thanksgiving in your heart. The wheat helps us to focus on the people who have faith in God but still have lawlessness in their heart. Offer them "Open Eyes" to see new beginnings so God can come in and do new things.

"I WILL BE KING OVER YOU"
Ezekiel 20:33-38

As I live, said he Lord God, surely with a mighty hand, and outstretched arm, and with wrath poured out, will I be king over you. I will bring you into the wilderness of the people and there I will enter into judgement with you face to face. I will make you pass under the rod and I will bring you into bond of the covenant. Larry had a dream he was in a field and God was speaking to him, then he was washed away by a flood of water. God was letting him know that he will stretch his arms around you and speak with you face to face, then he will wash all your sins away. The Lord restored Israel and washed away their sins and told them; Go serve everyone, of you his idols now and hereafter, if you will not listen to me or honor my holy name you shall no more profane me with your gifts and idols. Speak God's word with "Open Eyes" and he will manifest his holiness among you.

"HE WILL FIGHT OUR BATTLES"
1 Chronicles 5:20-22

And, when they prevailed over them the Hagrites and all who were with them were given into their hands, for they cried out to God in the battle and he granted their urgent plea because they trusted in him. For many feels because the war was of God and they lived in their place until the exile, we as people cannot fight all our battles, but God can in the natural and the Spiritual. If you trust in him when you call on him he will hear your cry. A lot of times we go through the storm a lot longer than expected all because we have no faith or little faith we fail to look through "Open Eyes" in the Spirit. Our family is fasting for a battle that is coming but because we trust God, he will see us through it when the time occurs we will be able to conquer the enemy and gain victor once again. Warriors of God will be prevailed in the midst of a war, because He will fight our battles.

13

THE
EYEWITNESS

"THE EYEWITNESS"
Act 2:32

This Jesus, God raised up and for that we all are witnesses. Jesus was not killed but he was crucified and resurrected from the dead to be glorified. Everyone has a pass that they can surely say they're not proud of, but we can go to Jesus and ask for forgiveness. He can use us with "Open Eyes" to do his will. Jesus has witnesses to show that he was raised up into the heavens. Look at it like this, all the people of your pass who know how you where before you meet Christ are your witness that when they see you now and see the mighty hand of God has changed you it brings them into faith to believe that Jesus is real. Be a witness to the unbelievers and help the believers to surrender so that you can show them how to build a bridge towards freedom through Christ Jesus. He who heals, delivers and set free.

"CHRISTIAN FELLOWSHIP"
Philemon 1:4

I thank God always when I remember you in my prayers. When you pray don't be selfish and pray for things just for your own gain. There are tons of others in need of prayer in this world we live in. Take times out to pray for a neighbor or a co-worker or even the lady at the store you see every day. Somethings can't be solved with money, but prayer can change things every time. Instead of beaten a person down about how they conduct their selves pray for them, talk to them about "Open Eyes" for God. Cry out to the Lord on their behalf and have real Christian fellowship with one another to encourage them to seek after God to renew their minds and create in them a clean spirit, that they may worship in spirit and in truth. Go to them and let them know that all they must do is call on Jesus and he will be there because he is a devoted friend indeed.

"RETURN IT TO MY ADDRESS"
1 Corinthian 11:17

But in the following instructions I do not commend you, because when you come together it is not for the better but for the worse. Jesus died for our sins so that there wouldn't be any condemnations for us because he bore all our sins on the cross. The Lord's Supper represents the blood Jesus shed and the bread his body as a living sacrifice and his resurrection gives us faith to know and strengthen us as believers that soon one day He will come and save us from all sin. Surround yourself with other believers so that when you are feeling weary your fellow sister or brother in Christ can come and encourage you to finish the race and to be strong and steadfast until Jesus returns. Look through "Open Eyes" that you may return and see the true spirit of God working in your life.

14

PRIDE ALMOST TOOK MY BLESSING

"PRIDE ALMOST TOOK MY BLESSING"
Ezekiel 7:24

I will bring the worst of the nations to take possession of their houses. I will put an end to the pride of the strong, and their holy places shall be profaned. Sometimes we let our pride get in the way of our blessings. If you know you need help and the source to our problem or situation can be resolved by asking for HELP, then open up your mouth and release your petition; because all of us have walked in humility at one point in time in our lives. Rather it was asking for help from the church, family, friends or even if you were co-parenting. The person we lease expect to give maybe the one that God has touched their hearts the most. I have leaned that you have not because you ask not. Let go of your pride through "Open Eyes" and let God prove to you the doubt is wrong; and He is still Mighty and Strong!!!

"SNOOTY PEOPLE"
Amos 4:1

Hear this Word, you cause of Bashan, who are on the mountain of Samaria, who oppress the poor, who crush the needy, who say to your husband; Bring that we may drink. Women who are partnered with their husband in leadership should be very careful about what it is you desire your husbands to do. A man will do anything to please his wife, even if he knows it might hurt him in the future. God wants us to have the finer things, but he doesn't want us to hinder others just to get what we want. "Open Eyes" will help you not use possessions as a weapon to fight against the oppressed. So, wives appreciate the gifts from your husbands, rather big or small, because it's not about how much he spent but the thought behind the gift that really matters. And if you desire to share your lavish things, give gracefully and not begrudged for God knows your heart.

"CORRECTIONS AND A DISTORTED VIEW"
2 Samuel 12:4

Now there came a traveler to the rich man, and he was unwilling to take one of his own flock or herd to prepare for the guest who had come to him, but he took the poor man's lamb and prepared it for the man who had come to him. Never take advantage of others, and if you need to offer or give constructive criticism toward others; make sure the other party can handle that criticism. Think about what you are going to say when correcting others and if the time is even right to address that issue, because after committing a sin for a long time it becomes repetitious and births more problems. Having "Open Eyes" will help you see that someone else's hick-ups or hang-ups may just as well be your own struggles; so, don't be bias towards yourself when confronted but better yet, take a self-examination and apply the same wisdom you dish out to others toward yourself.

15

FLATTERED BUT NOT FOOLED

"FLATTERED BUT NOT FOOLED"
Genesis 39:8

But he refused and said to his master's wife, "Behold, because of me my master has no concern about anything in the house, and he has put everything that he has in my charge." How can God manifest the fruits of your labor if you don't trust Him? "Open Eyes" will keep you from being enticed by the enemy when he tells you to do things your way because you feel you are in a safe zone. Resist the enemy even if it feels safe and ask God to let His will be done and not yours. You have the Authority over yourself and everything you do; use your power wisely!!! God already knows the plans he has for you, all you must do is trust the Holy Spirit and do what is pleasing to God and not man. Do not entertain wickedness, it will cause you to sin against God.

"THIS MEANS WAR"
Matthew 12:29

Oh, how can someone enter a strongman's house and plunder his goods, unless he first binds the strongman? Then indeed he may plunder his house. God has given us authority over the enemy and all satanic forces but if you are not in your rightful position to slay him then the enemy will come in and dismantle you and destroy your temple. You must guard your emotions, integrity, and character at all times; keeping "Open Eyes" to apprehend Satan's attack on your life. For the battle is not yours but it's the Lords. Spiritual warfare comes when you're going to a new level. "New Levels-New Devils." Prayer is your weapon of reproach towards the enemy. Don't back down but believe that victory is already in your favor from the beginning.

"DON'T BELIEVE IN FAIRY TALES"
2 Kings 21:18

And, Manasseh slept with his fathers, and was buried in the garden of his own house, in the garden of Uzza, and Amon his son, reigned in his place. You cannot say that you honor God but worship the devil by doing whatever your flesh desires. Often people build up their own god's and they began to believe that the way of their own practice of sacrifice is truth. Now in reality there is only one True Living God that we serve, and we come to the Father in spirit and in truth through holiness and righteousness. We must have "Open Eyes" to prepare our hearts to be committed and to walk up right according to his statues and commands. Fasting and praying is not to be taken lightly as an everyday ritual but it's to be done with honesty and loyalty of heart. Repent and put no other gods before our Lord and Savior Jesus Christ; whom was and is and is to come.

16

SPIRIT

AWAKENING

"SPIRIT AWAKENING"
Ezra 2:43

The Temple servants; the sons of Ziha, the sons of Hasupha, and the son of Tabbaoth, as with them; God wants to free us from a Babylon mind-set. So, have "Open Eyes" to see so you don't slip into a comfort zone that can cause you a set-back on your journey to your God given promise. How can a temple ever be built if you continue to stop along the process? In this life there are challenges and you must press through. Stay persistent and consistent in every area of your life. Ask the Holy Spirit to help you with your infirmities of weakness. If the enemy can get you off focus of what God has promised you, then you will allow yourself not to get to your destiny. Your blessings await you. How bad do you want them? Repent! Acknowledge your sin and restoration will take place giving you the ability to fulfill your assignments.

"GOD'S SUPERVISION"
2 King 6:1

Now the sons of the prophets said to Elisha, "See the place where we dwell under your charge is too strait for us. Sometimes we let life get the best of us and allow our flesh to over rail the Spirit when it should be the opposite. Do things out of the kindness of your heart and don't look for anything in return. As a believer we are to walk by faith and not by sight. We should gravitate to "Open Eyes" in the spirit because God wants to show his care and provision for those who trust in him. Even in our insignificant wants of everyday life God is always present. So, don't let the things you do for others allow you to forget who you are doing them for. We are all servants of the Almighty! Caring is the provisions of what is necessary for the health, welfare, maintenance and protections of someone or something.

"THE 7TH DAY"

Isaiah 58:13

If you turn back your foot from the Sabbath from doing your pleasure on my Holy day, and call the Sabbath a delight, and the holy day of the Lord honorable? If you honor it; not going your own way or seeking your own pleasure, or taking idols? But keep the Sabbath Day Holy; then shall you delight yourself in the Lord, and I will make you to ride upon the high places of the earth; and feed you with the heritage of Jacob; for the mouth of God has spoken. exercise "Open Eyes" by keeping the Sabbath Day Holy which is important because it shows God that you reverence His commands. And, after being Spiritually refilled around other believers it helps bring courage and hope to carry out your journey of life. Families can come together and unify, making it harder for the enemy to come in with discord. So, rest, reflect and give God praise on the 7th day.

17

MYSELF GOT IN THE WAY

"MYSELF GOT IN THE WAY"
Jeremiah 50:29

Summon archers against Babylon, all those who bend the bow. Encamp around her, let no one escape. Repay her according to her deeds, do to her according to all that she has done. For she has proudly defiled the Lord, the Holy One of Israel. As a Christian you come to realize through "Opened Eye's" that you are nothing without God. No boxer can become a champion on his own, but he must have a personal trainer. The Holy Spirit is our personal trainer, he gives us guidance and shows us how to have characteristics of Christ. The Holy Spirit also shows us how to be humble by praying in season and out of season. If you keep your eyes on the one who Blesses and not just the blessings it will make it harder for you to become self-centered and puffed up with self. Pride births arrogance and foolish infuriation, but God honors a humble servants heart.

18

THE
MYSTERY
OF HIS
WILL

"THE MYSTERY OF HIS WILL"
Ephesians 1:10

As a plan for the fullness of time to unite all things in him, things in heaven and things on earth. I believe God wants us all to come together; the believers with the unbelievers, the Muslim with the Catholic and the Jehovah witness alike; because God says that he loves us all. No matter what your religion is God say's, "ever knee shall bow, and every tongue shall confess that I am Lord". Therefore, have "Open Eyes" to see and know the goodness of God, because rather you love the Lord or fear His power, you will bow to him. God's purpose and will is though his word. There are things in our lives that we don't understand but we must trust and believe and have faith and let God show us who he is through his Word being performed. Somethings are not to be understood until the return of the King.

19

SILENT CRIES OUTWARD SMILES

"SILENT CRIES OUTWARD SMILES"
Jeremiah 9:10

I will take up weeping and wailing for the mountains, and lamentation for the pastures of the wilderness, because they are laid waste so that no one passes through, and the voice of cattle is not heard. Both the birds of the air and the beast have fled and are gone. Jesus showed us Agape Love when he was on the way to be crucified on the cross with compassion towards those who were persecuting Him. Although many lied and were deceitful he still said forgive them for they know not what they do. And, as leaders in the body of Christ it gets hard when we know the Sins of many that they to betray us. It's always a constant battle between Sin and Righteousness, but we are to hate the Sin and love the person. The Holy Spirit will cause those things that are in the darkness to come into his marvelous light. Lord teach us to have spiritual "Open Eyes" to love as you love.

"NEVER JUDGE A BOOK BY ITS COVER"
Acts 10:9

Never judge a book by its Cover. The next day as they were on their journey and approaching the city, Peter went up on the house top about the sixth hour to pray. You might work or attend a church that has a lot of turmoil in it. Blacks don't like whites, this woman don't like that one, one is lazy the other is foolish, one is out spoken the other has to many personal issues; whatever the problem may be know that we are all as filthy rags in God's eye. But through His word, God says we can all come to him for repentance of our sins and be changed. Sometimes things appear that the situation looks hopeless, but if we keep "Open Eyes" on him, God will come and turn it around and give us the hope and faith to come to him, so we can be cleansed as white as snow and made clean from the inner to the outer core, so, never judge a book by its cover.

"THE WOMAN CAUGHT IN ADULTERY"
John 8:11

She said, "No one Lord!" And, Jesus said, "Neither do I condemn you; go and from now on sin no more." The men caught the women in adultery and wanted to stone her but our Lord, Jesus, the Son of man, told them if any of you have no sin upon your head, then you cast the first stone, and none could answer; all they could do was walk away. This means that just because someone has committed a sin you still have to be careful not to judge them because when you point your finger at someone, you always have 3 pointing back at you. With "Open Eyes" check yourself, because Jesus died for us all and it is he, and he alone who can judge us, but instead pray for your sister and brother, and speak life and not death into their situation, because Jesus said, "I came not to condemn, but that you may have life and life more abundantly."

20

AM
I ALLOWED
TO
SPEAK

"AM I ALLOWED TO SPEAK"
Philippians 2:4

Let each of you look not only to his own interest but also to the interest of others. In the body of Christ there are so many talents and ideas from so many people. As leaders you must always keep an open mind-set with "Open Eyes" before you because there are always different opinions from others. If you have a one-track mind and always saying to others "it is my way or no way" this breaks down the unity and core of a strong foundation. Take the time out to let your husband, wife, children or others speak what they think in conversations and began to see how the lines of communication will open clear to other's feelings or understanding. Humility and Unity strengthens us from selfishness, jealousy and division. Genuine people show interest in other believers and maintain healthy relationships.

21

I

PROSPERED

IN MY

LOST

"I PROSPERED IN MY LOST"
Act 9:31

So, the church throughout all Judea and Galilee and Samaria had peace and was being built up. And walking in the fear of the Lord and in the comfort of the Holy Spirit it multiplied. A little leaven leaves the whole lump. One corrupt person that is in the church, job, family, etc.. can ruin it for everyone else. Ask God to help you discern with "Open Eyes" who is for you or against you. We must sometimes loose in order to gain what's for us. The adversary only comes to steal, kill and destroy the plans of our Lord. Where there is no purification through the Divine person of the Holy Spirit; one can only appear to bring forth edification. But, good people bring good vibes to prosper in Faith, Hope and Love. God wants to take away that which is unjust, so he can fill you with that which is right and just!!! Hold on to that which is good, that you may prosper in all you do.

"MY ROCK"
Luke 4:28

He is like a man building a house, who dug deep and laid the foundation on the rock. And when a flood arose, the stream broke against that house and could not shake it because it had been well built. Obey God and trust in him that if he gives you instructions for your life; he knows what's best for you. Therefore, when a crisis rises-up in your relationship, stand firm and be unmovable; because God says, "if you love me you will obey my commands, I will protect you and keep you from falling". So, trust in the Lord and always do good, and with "Open Eyes" remember your Covent with the Lord because Satan's mission is to take you out, and if you don't serve the Lord personally then there is no way you can have him fight your battles for you. Keep His steadfast love in your heart because he will never leave you or forsake you.

"HE WOULD BRING THE PEOPLE OUT OF EGYPT"
Ezekiel 20: 27-32

The Lord your God swore saying he would bring the people out of Egypt and promised to give them a land flowing with milk and honey; the most glorious of all lands which means he will deliver you from evil and save you and bring you to your promise land. Where there is nothing, but good fruit of awesome nectar grown. It is the Most high of the High. But, don't defile yourself with Idols or any other gods, for this is a sign of rebellion to disobey the Lord. But instead, have "Open Eyes" to see what the Lord is doing to prosper you. Today was the first day Larry and I went and Evangelized to four different people, and it felt good to pray for the people. We then topped it off with an Awesome night at TBN. I encourage you to always walk in the way of the Lord, keep His status and obey His laws always, by doing this He will bless you and cause you to prosper.

22

HEART
CRY

"HEART CRY"
Psalm 24:9

Lift up your heads, O ye gates!!! And lift them up, O ancient doors that the King of Glory may come in. Who is the King of Glory? Our God he is the king of Glory. Lord, thank you for opening my heart so that I may love you and worship you no matter how things may seem. Let me take the time today to let you know that you are my everything. It's because of you I am in my right mind. Be transparent and cry out to the Father and tell him you need him, and you want the Holy Spirit to come in your life and direct you on what you should do. Growing pains hurt but it strengthens us for battle. God hears our cry and wants us to trust in Him with every circumstance of our lives. Worship distracts the enemy and confuses him. Ask God to allow His Holy Spirit to come into your temple and began to let his joy and peace overwhelm you to the depths of your soul. Lord, help us to have "Open Eyes" to see your glory.

23

I'M
IN
NO RUSH

"I'M IN NO RUSH"
1 Corinthians 7:32

I want you to be free from anxieties. The unmarried person is anxious about the things of the Lord. How to please the Lord, because lust can cause us to give into the flesh desires of wanting a man or woman to give us attention emotionally and physically. But, if you don't love the Lord, what happens is soul ties can come into action and you'll be wondering how you fell in love with a person who don't really love you. If you are single, ask God to feel those voided areas with his presence, and in your waiting-season draw near to the Lord and he will draw near to you. Have "Open Eyes" for the Lord and put your trust in Him so you don't lead yourself into temptation to sin to a temporary fix that can affect you a lifetime. Open your mind and heart to see how he is making you into the person that he has called you to be, and all other things will be added.

"IT'S ONLY A MIRAGE"
Mark 13:4-6

Tell us when will these things be and what will be the sign when all these things are about to be accomplished? And Jesus began to say to them, see that no one leads you astray. Many will come in my name saying I am he! And they will lead many astray. Be careful that you ask God for a discerning spirit on who people are because a lot of folk will come up to you and say God told them they were to tell you something; are to do something, and if you're not careful you will fall into Satan's snare. Therefore, Jesus says do not be anxious beforehand; what you are to say, but say whatever is given you in that hour, for it is not you who speak but the Holy Spirit. See with "Open Eyes" because Wolves come in sheep clothing therefore; always consult God first in all that you do, and you will know if it's sent from the Lord or the adversary.

"DISAPPEARING ACT"
John 7:35

The Jews said to one another, where does this man intend to go that we will not find him? Does he intend to go to the Dispersion among the Greeks, and teach the Greeks? Jesus sent his comforter which is the (Holy Spirit) to help lead and guide us down the path of righteousness. The assurance of the Holy Ghost lets you know that the Lord is dwelling in you, but we must always remember that even if you can't feel God's presence you still must have faith and trust in him. Have "Open Eyes" and the Holy Spirit will instruct you on what to do. Don't look for feelings to determine if you're doing right. But believe and receive in this gift that doesn't have a Designated time to come or go but will always be with you once you are born again in the Spirit.

24

NO
PLACE
FOR
INDIFFERENCE

"NO PLACE FOR INDIFFERENCE"
Amos 6:1

Woe to those who are at ease in Zion and to those who feel secure on the mountain of Samaria, the notable men of the first of the nations to whom the house of Israel comes! Have you lost heart of your assignment in the Kingdom of God, and became selfish? Your wealth, favor, and blessings where designed for you to give back to the poor and needy not for self-indulgence. God has freely given to you so give back graciously. Some people miss out on opportunities to serve God's children because of their pride and ego. Keep "Open Eyes" and don't allow fame and fortune to take rule over your gift and abilities for His work. Because what God has called blessed; you could curse by living in complacency. Where one door is shut another door is open so that you may walk straight into it. He shows no partiality.

"JUSTICE WILL BE SERVED"

John 7:35

When an Ox gores a man or a woman to death, the Ox shall be stoned, and its flesh shall not be eaten; but the owner of the Ox shall not be liable. God will require each person to be held accountable for their own actions. No one has the right to kill another human being. It's a sin and God is against it. God created man in the image of himself, so if you take someone's life and commit murder you have broken his commandment. He will see you and a penalty must be paid; and justice will be served. humans are not animals and we shouldn't be treated as such. Mankind, has the opportunity to God's eternal life; not animals. Therefore, having "Open Eyes" will help you see clearly how to treat others, as you would want to be treated, remembering he created each of us in His own image.

"CALL OF DUTY"

Numbers 4:23

From thirty years old up to fifty years old, you shall list them, all who can come to duty. To do service is the tent of meeting. Through "Open Eyes" you can see there is no I in team. We as brothers and sisters of Christ must learn to come together and help one another in the Church. No line of service is bigger than the next person's. God wants true worshipers and servants who don't mind going the extra mile to help in the work of the Father. Leaders must always keep good lines of communication with others this way strong relationships can be built on a solid foundation. The labor can be overwhelming at times but in the end, God gets the Glory from your faithfulness towards Him. Always serve with a humble heart and know that you are working for the Lord.

25

MERE

RITUALS

"MERE RITUALS"
Hosea 8:13

As for my sacrificial offerings they sacrifice flesh and eat it, but the Lord does not accept them now, he will remember their iniquity and punish their sins and they shall return to Egypt. God wants us to pray and fast often, but he does not want it to become a form of informality denying the power there of. You can have a poverty mindset even though you no longer live physically in a poverty-stricken place. Moses had to renew his mind after he disobeyed God and struck the rock instead of speaking to the rock. The Israelites lost trust in God after being in the wilderness. We cannot go into our wealthy place with old mindsets and unforgiveness. God has not dealt with us according to our iniquities and we should not do it to others. "Open Eyes" can change you from your ritual patterns and devote your hearts to His desires of wholesomeness.

"SHE REJECTED MY PROPOSAL"
Deuteronomy 28:28

The Lord will strike you with madness and blindness and confusion of mind. No one knows what Our Father is going to do or how He is going to do it, but we do understand him (Jesus) to some degree. You cannot let your circumstances allow you to be dismayed, depressed or discouraged because of how it looks but know that God has placed you where he wants you to be. But if you are disobedient and choose not to follow His will, He will turn you over to your depraved mind. So, I encourage you to have "Open Eyes" for the Spirit and do what is right unto the Lord your God. If not, you will find yourself walking around mad at things that's going on around you for no reason; blind that you can't see Satan's snares or the pathway in which he is trying to take you down to corrupt your life.

"DELAY DON'T MEAN DENIAL"

1 Samuel 1:7

So, it went on year by year. As often as she went up to the house of the Lord, she provoked her. Therefore, Hannah wept and would not eat. Sometimes we try to judge others according to what their circumstances are but what the human eye can't see is that God is changing them on the inside. The outer appearance can fool others, but God knows the heart. If you see your neighbor in need of a helping hand. Pray with them and give them encouraging words that will help give them hope to active their faith. And, if you ask for something and it hasn't come to pass at your expected time; remember that you shouldn't give up, but trust in the Lord always. If, He said it, then he will do it, and it will come to pass by and by; and with "Open Eyes" you will see His perfect timing is always right on time.

26

WHAT
IS
YOUR
REQUEST

"WHAT IS YOUR REQUEST"
Ester 5:4

And, Esther said, "If it pleased the King, let the King and Haman come today to a feast that I have prepared for the King." The favor of God is so unspeakable and not imaginable to the eye sight. The Lord our King will grant us favor when we obey him. If you ask, then you shall receive. Favor is far more better then silver or gold. Some people have favor among the sight of man but the favor we should all want is God's favor. Overflow has no limit in the sight of God. Intercede for someone else and watch what God does as he intercedes for you. Don't worry about what, when and where; just know that the King...the Lord, He is the King of Glory!!! And, always have "Open Eyes" for others, then God will say, "what is your request" and it shall be granted unto you. Favor, on top of favor from the Lord our King.

27

FAITH
TO
CALL
IT OUT

"FAITH TO CALL IT OUT"
Matthew 9:32

As they were going away behold, a demon possessed man who was mute was brought to him, and when the demon was cast out, the dumb man spoke. Spiritual "Open Eyes" can see that demons are evil Spirits that are controlled by Satan. Demonic spirits know who Jesus is, but they think they do not have to obey him. If you find yourself or others, physically, mentally or spiritually, demon possessed then you will see traits of distortion being done to yourself or others. It's like a puppet master pulling the strings of a puppet to do what he wants it to do. Satan will try to lure you into suicide or death or even to kill someone else. But by the power and authority of Jesus Christ, demons can be cast out of people. Faith in Jesus is the beginning of Hope. When you act on your faith and trust in Jesus you will have the assurance of Salvation and the power over drunkenness, lust, seizures, cancer, high-blood pressure, and all manner of wickedness, sickness and diseases will have to go and be cast out and healed, because the Bible says, "we wrestle not against flesh and blood, but against principalities, against powers, against the rulers of the darkness of this world, and against spiritual wickedness in high places, but through Christ Jesus, and him sharing his blood on the cross for our sakes, we can be healed, and this is the assurance we have in Him.

"SAUL WAS JEALOUS OF DAVID"
I Samuel 23: 6-14

Saul was jealous of David, but David knew that Saul wanted to kill and destroy him. David ask the Lord, "is Saul trying to harm me?" And the Lord said, "Yes." David then at that time escaped Keilah and went wherever he could go. God will show you who your enemies are if you ask him. So, have "Open Eyes" in the spirit to what He is showing you. Trust and believe in God alone; and then, and only then, will He be able to hide you away from your enemies. God will watch over you in every way and no harm will come your way. Jealously, envy and strife are of the adversary and his plan is to kill, steal and destroy. But God!!! He will not give you over unto his hands and fear not, because if God is for you, that it better than the whole world against you. He will allow you to rest in his arms and give you peace.

28

I

GIVE

YOU MY

YES

"I GIVE YOU MY YES"
Deuteronomy 28:25

The Lord will cause you to be defeated before your enemies. You shall go out one way against them and flee seven ways before them. And you shall be a dishonor to all the kingdoms of the earth. Disobedience can cause you to not be able to grow spiritually to your full potential. Your blessings are not given to you because you are gifted in many areas, but they come from your obedience to God. You have to stay focused on God's plan for your life. The enemy wants you to feel overwhelmed with problems, troubles, and with many obstacles to make you feel as if there is no hope. Disobedient brings curses but obedience brings blessing; therefore, you must ask the Holy Spirit to help you with your infirmities because where you are weak, I am strong. Remember, God knows the best plan for your life, and with "Open Eyes" you can have full control (through the spirit) to walk into your destiny. He will say "Yes" to you if you line up with his will and honor his ways.

"RICH MAN POOR MAN"
Deuteronomy 28:30

You shall betroth a wife, but another man shall ravish her. You shall build a house, but you shall not dwell in it. You shall plant a vineyard, but you shall not enjoy the fruit. Often people take for granted the things God has blessed them with, it's not until he takes it away that we began to realize that He was the one who provided you with all your needs. Homeless people are human beings just like you and me. And just because they are poor it doesn't mean that they're lazy or looking for a handout. There are people who work every day but are still poor. Justice must be served. The Bible says that God rains on the just and the unjust, the rich and the poor man. Help society by going the extra mile for someone less fortunate then yourself and choose to have "Open Eyes" in the spirit and watch God bless you beyond measure.

"DO YOU BELIEVE"

John 3:36

Whoever believes in the Son has eternal life; whoever does not obey the Son shall not see life, but the wrath of God remains on him. Jesus says that those who believe in him will have everlasting life. So, I encourage you to have "Open Eyes" that you may see clearly how to join up with God, so you can receive eternal life. Remember, we all are born into sin therefore, we must be born again; rebirthed in Christ. Jesus wants us to trust that he knows what is best for us. For it is He who sits high on the throne and no-one can come to the Father except through Jesus. Therefore, we must believe in Him and then, and only then can we receive everlasting life in the Kingdom, there shall we rest in his promises and know that he is God; today, tomorrow and forevermore.

29

YOU

WILL

WIN

"YOU WILL WIN"
1 Samuel 13:22

So, on the day of battle there was neither sword nor spear found in the hand of any of the people with Saul and Jonathan, but with Saul and Jonathan his son had them. God can use the enemy's own weapons against them to conquer the battle. Your sickness can bring healing through the Word of God which is your sword. Your strength comes from the Lord if you call on Him for help, he will come and rescue you. Safety is the confidence of God's hope and present help in the time of own troubles against the oppressor. The battle is not yours but the Lord's, so let God go to war for you and keep silent and you will come out on top all the time. Oppositions may occur, and some challenges are trying, But God is you strong tower in whom shall you be afraid. I will build a fence around you and protect you on every side says the Lord; And you will Win!!!!

"FATHER KNOWS BEST"
Matthew 7:11

If you then who are evil, know how to give good gifts to your children how much more will your father who is in heaven give good things to those who ask him. When we pray the Lord hears our cry and behold what manner of love the Father has bestowed on us, that we should be called children of God. He listens to our request and makes the decision if we should have it then, later, are not at all. He truly does loves us with an everlasting love; therefore, If I ask for a Mercedes Benz but he knows I can't even afford to fix it if it breaks down and it could very well become a hindrance on me; He may say no, but it's because he knows what is best for me. So, as we seek him through faith with "Open Eyes" we will learn that His divine power has given us everything we need for life and godliness through our knowledge of Him who called us by His own glory and goodness.

"KNOWLEDGE AND GOOD JUDGEMENT"

2 Chronicles 9:23

And, all the kings of the earth sought the presence of Solomon to hear his wisdom which God had put into his mind. Solomon asked God for wisdom and not for riches or wealth of the land, but because he asked God for wisdom God gave him wealth, riches, and honor as well. We should always put God first in everything we do and then everything will be added to it. God wants to bless us with his best but when he does he wants to make sure we keep what he blessed us with. If you have wisdom alone with "Open Eyes" you will know how to keep what you have. Keep God as your number one priority and learn to be content with what you have, and you will have greater wealth than you could every accumulate. Store up your treasure in heaven not on earth, love him and trust him because God has never forsaken those who seek him.

30

EVERLASTING

GOD

"EVERLASTING GOD"
Lamentations 3:15

He has filled me with bitterness; he has sated me with wormwood. If God never did anything else for me pertaining to the tangible things here on earth. I Would still be faithful to serve Him? When I'm in a toil place coming out of a dry season and it appears there is no light at the end of a dark tunnel. I Remember that Jesus Christ's love will never fail or forsake me. My hope and strength come from my creator who desires for me to have peace and steadfast Love. It's clearly to see with "Open Eyes" that after every big storm there is a rainbow that represents God's promise. Remove my afflictions Lord and honor my petition of forgiveness. I will be faithful unto you until my judgment day. How great is your mercy and steadfast love towards me? How great is your mercy LORD; for your LOVE endureth Forever.

31

SEVEN
FOLDS'

"SEVEN FOLDS'"
Amos 9:15

I will plant them on their land and they shall never again be uprooted out of the land that I have given them says the Lord your God. Our lives should reflect the image of Jesus Christ. When obstacles come our way ask God how should we handle this situation? The fruits of the Spirit are manifested when we allow the Holy Spirit to have full control over our life. So, through Love, joy, peace, patience, kindness, goodness, faithfulness, gentleness, and self-control we have "Open Eyes" to see in the spirit; therefore, we can identify and see the distractions clearly that we may get to the root of the problem and fix the mistakes we have made in past situations; remembering that God will restore us and he will give back everything the enemy stole. To be rewarded by the Father is much greater than anything this world could

---

ever offer. God demonstrates His own love toward us in that while we were yet still sinners, Christ died for us and purchased our freedom with His own blood; and the faithful love of the LORD never ends. His mercies never cease. Great is His faithfulness; His mercies begin afresh each morning...The LORD is good to those who depend on Him, to those who search for Him. Thank God for his promises and that His, words are always yes and Amen!!!

MARKEDA JOHNSON

OPEN EYE'S DAILY DEVOTIONAL

Made in the USA
Columbia, SC
06 November 2018